ARE YOU THE ONE?

LYDIA F. BEST

Unless otherwise indicated, all Scripture quotations are taken from the Holy Bible, King James Version.

ISBN: 9798392230686

Contact Information:
Dr. Lydia B. Best, RN, MS, FNP, DMin
Certified Health and Wellness Coach
Inspired To Be Ministries
P.O. Box 30495
Greenville, NC 27836
LydiaBest777@gmail.com

Dedication

To human beings all over the world who dream of a better world and have what it takes to make it happen! That means YOU if you are reading this dedication. You matter, you are significant, you have a voice worth sharing, and you are guaranteed to experience better if you adhere to the recommendations given by the one who created us all. It's your choice. Determine your future with intentionality and let your actions represent the greatness in you!

Table of Contents

Preface

I first got the idea of the title for this book after attending a professional conference and hearing some awful stories about professionals who treat other newly graduated 'professionals' as well as other seasoned 'professionals' who are of different cultures and ethnicities with hate and contempt in the workplace! And the sad thing is, these professionals are in so called 'helping professions', caring for the sick and less fortunate individuals who are trusting these 'professionals' to make them well and experience wholeness. And I thought, who is going to make these 'sick professionals' well? These people with their 'holier than thou attitudes' who form cliques on the job and place pettiness and minor differences (often created by Almighty God) above the care for humanity who instills trust in them for care??? They are adult (at least in age) bullies! The saddest part is that this type of behavior has been carried from generation to generation at the expense of VARIOUS

PROFESSIONS and POLITICS! This behavior is destructive, disrespectful, and must be stopped.

So, the question came to my mind, who will be the one to bring an end to this saga? Who will be the one to say enough is enough? Who will be the one to stop contributing to the problem and begin to solve the problem? And then came the overwhelming question...ARE YOU THE ONE? The spirit of entitlement, of self-seeking disdain has permeated the world and makes our systems dysfunctional. There seems to be no quality control measures enforced or if they are, they are flawed profusely. And so, I, believing in the power of ONE, decided to embrace my perceptions and look at some basic ingrained concepts entangled in the spirituality of man's existence and the historical indoctrination of man which begins with the institution of family. It may seem a little twisted to some but bear with me and let us reason together as you answer the question in the pursuit of better relationships and a better world, "ARE YOU THE ONE?"

It does not take a Rocket Scientist to see that we live in a broken world, a society where wholeness is rare, if it even exists. But I have to believe that it does exist somewhere and that somewhere is the place where the presence of God reigns. There is no lack of negativity, hatred, poverty, jealousy, anxiety, stress, or poor health; hence, it can become difficult for us to see beyond the black clouds of injustice and inequality that plagues our society like a never-ending plague. Yet, there is hope!

It is imperative and important that we seriously ask ourselves, "Why are we in the state, the condition, in which we find ourselves?" What is the main desire of our heart?" "What can we do to change things for the better?" I want to challenge each of us to ponder these three questions as a combined focal point, so to speak, as we delve into the pages of this book which I have been inspired by God to pen. It's been a long time coming, as the song goes, but a change IS coming, and the essence of change is within each of us. We are not meant to live in a bubble alone, wrestling with the challenges we all face. We need to unite and help one another to defeat the foe that threatens us all. It is past time for us to stop complaining about the brokenness of our existence and decide to use our creative abilities to mend the brokenness which is so very prevalent no matter where we turn. If I may, and I give myself permission, let me now remind us all of a passage of scripture from the Bible which many of us are somewhat familiar: "If my people, which are called by my name, shall humble themselves and pray, and seek my face, and turn from their wicked ways; then will I hear from heaven, and will forgive their sin, and will heal their land." (2 Chronicles 7:14, KJV)

Historically we can look at the scriptures, including the above passage, as just that, 'HISTORY'. But it becomes more when you acknowledge the fact that God changes not, history repeats itself, and if God delivered someone in the past who had the same or similar problem as I am facing or experiencing today, He can and will do the same for me NOW! Look at what happened in the days of old and also remember, 'there is nothing new under the sun'. God's promises are true, and it is our responsibility to exercise the measure of faith which each of us has been given in order to successfully complete our earthly journey and move on to the eternal life God has prepared for us. This earth is not our home; however, we are to take care of God's property, His creation, with the guidance of Holy Spirit, turning to God and resisting the devil every step of the way.

We were created to worship God, our Creator, the King of Heaven and Earth, our Heavenly Father. We can trace the evil that entered the hearts of men back to the Garden of Eden. Sadly, far too many of us human beings use this 'fall' as an excuse and are quickly to place blame on someone or something for our sinful behaviors and therefore take on an 'I can't help it' attitude instead of acknowledging God and asking Him to give us the knowledge, wisdom, and understanding that we need to fight the good fight of faith and be victorious over every temptation and form of wickedness. Because of Jesus, we can have authority over the flesh, but we must take it by force **spiritually** and we will witness how our bonding to Jesus Christ materializes to be exceedingly, abundantly, above all we could ask or think! (Ephesians 3:20 KJV)

ARE YOU THE ONE who will do the will of God and change the trajectory of this broken world, or will you persist in ignorance and foolishness, constrained to murmuring, and complaining about the obvious while the obvious you think is the normal is just a façade begging for interventions to a better life for you and your neighbors? **ARE YOU THE ONE?**

Purpose

The purpose of this book is to invoke through questioning, an action, or actions by you, the reader, that will positively improve the status of the world in which we live, making the world healthier and representative of the Godly Heritage belonging to us all. I beg of you to THINK, ASK QUESTIONS, GET ANSWERS, MAKE APPROPRIATE CHOICES contributing toward true justice, real love, true compassion, kindness, and a work ethic that demonstrates the will of God which makes all of this and More possible for the benefit of CHILDREN OF WORTH whom we are; not by our own merit, but by the unmerited FAVOR OF GOD!

Read every word and take notes, journal, develop a plan of action for yourself and your family and act upon that plan. Don't just sit around and grope but move by the inspiration of God and prove to yourself that you are more than a conqueror. Change your words to change your world and develop positive statements/affirmations which you will speak aloud repetitiously. Remember faith comes by hearing and hearing by the word of God. Life and death are in the power of the tongue. Choose life! Utilize all of your working senses to the glory of God and remember, there is a balm in Gilead and our world can be healed. It's up to YOU!

Choices Today, Blessings Today And Tomorrow

The Bible tells us that a spiritual heritage, a godly heritage is vital in order for generations to experience the joy of the Lord and understand our purpose. Spiritual heritage binds us together. We must choose to live for God and empower our children and our children's children through the sharing our history. In sharing our history, we give hope, causing the remembrance of former things with the obvious interventions made by God. As we look back and see where the hand of God has kept us and protected us through the toughest of situations, our faith grows and we are able to persevere, knowing that God is on our side. Our heritage gives us a better understanding of our past and how we evolve into our present. Acknowledge God in every situation and directions come into being exactly as we need them and on time!

Unfortunately, too many households have existed without the trainings of God's Word and therefore, there is a lacking of purpose and faith. The cultural environment in which one grows has a profound influence on one's behavior across the life span. This is known as the epigenetics of one's existence. You cannot expect someone who never learned how to eat with a fork to go to some fancy restaurant, even if they dress the part, and proceed to eat baked chicken by cutting small pieces at a time, for example. Being used to eating EVERYTHING with the fingers, the person is more likely to dig into the plate hands first and proceed to feed themselves. Bad example? But you get the picture, I hope.

Another example, if you grew up in an environment where everyone looked out for themselves and cheated, stole, cussed all the time etc. and you never saw any other behaviors within your circle, not even on the TV shows you watched, what do you think will happen as you get older? Unless you are exposed to better and given the hope to be better and dream of better, repeated behaviors will ensue. But the good thing is, EPIGENETICS can be changed. DNA on the other hand, is here to stay but lifestyles can be favorably changed by intentionality and repetitious behaviors. Better choices can be made for more favorable and predictive outcomes.

Train up a child in the way he should go (Proverbs 22:6 KJV) is a warning to all parents and parent- figures. No child comes into the world knowing how to hate, cheat, steal, etc. Instead, a child comes as a gift from God, to be nourished and taught about the ONE who gives life to all that they may be a part of the Kingdom of God. You and your children are to use the talents, gifts, and abilities you possess to make the world more loving, compassionate, and kind while thriving in preparation for the next life. Children are referred to as being of the kingdom of heaven (Matthew 19:14). We must BE as little children, capable of being molded in the Potter's Hands. It's disgusting to think that some folks spend more time training or seeking training for their dogs and cats than they do their children. And yes, training cats???? I hear that's not really possible, but you get the idea, right?

In case you didn't know or have forgotten, all choices have consequences whether good or not so good; therefore, we must place carefully focused thought into our choices and intentionally choose what honors God. Things like serving, giving, helping others to be the best they can be, loving one another, leaving a valuable heritage not just monetarily but in morals and respect for generations to come are among ways to honor God. By the way we live, we can actualize blessings of mercy, seeing the grace of God in every situation. What other ways can you think of to honor God with your life?

It is not God's desire that we yield to the logismoi[1] attacks which can lead us to addictions, ungodly behaviors of all kinds, eventually resulting in turning away from

---

[1] I encourage you to research this word logismoi and find historical writings which go beyond the scope of this book.

and rejecting anything that has to do with God! Okay, I hear you asking, "what in the world is 'logismoi'?" Logismoi in the Greek is pronounced, lo-gee-smee or lo-yeez-mee. Logismoi (the plural of logismos), a term used to describe assaultive or tempting thoughts. These thoughts or thought images come to lead us away from Christ. They are distractions that can lead us to fall. If we don't shoo them away or demand that they cease, we can find ourselves in the grips of Satan. I'm so glad that the scriptures tell us that when we turn to God and resist the devil, the devil will flee from us! (James 4:7 KJV). The most powerful way to shoo 'logismoi flies' away is by using the living WORD OF GOD to rebuke and resist the enemy's attacks. Just know that the attacks will not cease as long as we are on this earth; hence, we must pray without ceasing and diligently seek God daily. Remember, we wrestle not against flesh and blood, but against principalities, against powers, against the rulers of the darkness of this world, against spiritual wickedness in high places (Ephesians 6:12 KJV). This wrestling represents what I call the 'logismoi dilemma'. You can be on your knees praying or sitting in the pulpit and those thoughts come out of nowhere.

Perhaps you remember the cartoons where on one shoulder of a character who is about to decide or choose to do something, sits an angel represented by a halo and on the other is a devil in red with a pitchfork and horns? Each shoulder presence is whispering in the ear of the character, trying to persuade him to do either right or wrong. Well, truth be told the devil may sometimes appear as an angel in your presence, so it is vitally important to know the voice of God. Knowing God's voice comes through spending quality time with Him in prayer, study of His Word and listening attentively to the preaching of His Word from Scripture readings. At any rate, life is choice driven and God gives us free will to make choices, but He guides us and always makes a way for us to escape bad situations (1 Corinthians 10:13 KJV). So, ARE YOU THE ONE to make good choices?

There is a lot of discussion today about having the proper "mindset". It can sound easy as it rolls off of the tongue, but the struggle is real! 'Without Jesus, we cannot make it through this life victoriously. But again, remember, we have instructions from the Bible, our life's manual. Colossians 3 explains clearly what we **should** do. And because repetition is how we learn, we find other passages of scripture which reiterate what and how we should respond to life's challenges. Read various versions of God's Word to understand the written word more clearly and always ask God to give you wisdom. What choices do you feel an urge to make today? Are YOU THE ONE who will choose wisely so that the Kingdom will be experienced in this earth? ARE YOU THE ONE with a treasure, a talent or gift that needs to be presented before Jesus and blessed to be a world changer? Humbly walking before the Lord, loving mercy, and doing justly in every aspect of life, showing that you are able to make a positive difference is just the beginning to effect great change for a better world - one step at a time.

Healthy Habits Create Strong Families

Too many homes are being destroyed at alarming rates because of poor habits and presuppositions often based on distorted views and planted seeds frequently stemming from television or social media. Prior to all of the technological advances which we now experience, homes were being destroyed by substitutes of various kinds as well, but things seem to have exploded. Very few families sit together at home for dinner or relax in the family room together to watch a show on television unless some still have 'MOVIE NIGHT'. Most homes have televisions and/or computers in each bedroom so if there **is** a shared meal, after it's over, everyone goes to their 'own space' or room. Some family members use their phones, at the dinner table even, to text each other when they are in close enough proximity to just talk! Simple talking as a form of communication is on the verge of becoming extinct or at least a rare commodity. The breakdown of the family has negatively impacted children, especially adolescents at an alarming rate as technology has advanced! Children have difficulty expressing themselves and there is exponential confusion. According to research, suicide rates have increased as well as criminal acts and substance abuse. Strife, jealousy, lack of commitment to the success of family growth and development, lack of genuine concern, wrong priorities, negative attitudes, and poor communication skills are among the culprits leading to destruction of the family. And you guessed it! Selfish has replaced selfless behaviors. If family units are being destroyed, down goes the community which is made up of FAMILIES and hence the world is tainted and broken.

Habits are acquired behaviors done over time repetitiously. If the habit is good, all is well but if the habit is not so good and leads to destruction, that is obviously undesirable. The old saying 'charity begins at home' is so full of truth. In the Bible, we see the word charity replaced with love, therefore being synonymous. And if we analyze deeper, we see that God is love; hence, God must be at the center of all families or else there is grave dysfunction as evidenced by divorce rates increasing over the decades, domestic violence, and chaos on many levels. In many instances, children are not sure of their identity and their roles within the family. How are members to be seen as contributing members of society? What are the contributions? Are contributions primarily positive or negative? Do you know who YOU are? Are you willing and able to help your loved ones answer these questions? Do you know to whom we all belong?

Families are as different as night and day, but each family has something in common. Each family is a system! A system consists of two or more parts so even an individual who considers himself a hermit, a loner, a unit of one, is still a system. The body of that one person has many features and many parts, organs, which work together. Let me remind you, we are fearfully and wonderfully made (Psalm 139:14 KJV). God took great care in making each of us, knowing us even before we were formed in our mother's womb, and we are actually made holy and set apart for God's use (Jeremiah 1:5 KJV; 1 Peter 1:15-16 and other scriptures KJV). We have some of the same basic needs, yet we are unique. We are all a part of the big picture, like a world-wide puzzle, a beautiful garden of flowers with different fragrances and abilities to brighten one's life! We are a bunch of 'me onlys" with more in common than we care to acknowledge. We have unique DNA and fingerprints, but we all need love, food, shelter, a sense of self-worth, water, exercise, sun, etc. The good thing about our needs is that God has already made provisions for each and every need. He has given someone the answer to every problem imaginable. If only we would get our systems to cooperate and work together for good and not evil, we would be better able to receive the exceedingly, abundantly, above rewards God has planned for us sooner than later. Use your voice as an oracle of God. ARE YOU THE ONE?

Within each family system, there are expectations. Some expectations may be considered strict and more focused than others, but there are expectations. Immediate environments are diverse and contribute to the manner in which a community and eventually the world functions and interacts on a daily basis. It is crucial that the family unit has structure and that each individual is trained to acceptably fit into the society and cultural mores. Consequences result from behaviors which are not accepted and can be deemed detrimental to the community or culture. Laws are set and enforced for the safety and justice of all; however, we know and have witnessed that there are many times when injustices are quite evident and legal actions must occur. We have seen and perhaps participated in riots or protests because of outrageous wrongs perpetrated upon human beings and animals too. Nevertheless, injustices may never be atoned, or it may take many years before justice is received. We know that there are inequalities around the world but that doesn't make it any easier to swallow. There is an ongoing battle in the arena of acceptable relationships, and it is safe to say that everyone has a part to play in the orchestration of harmony amongst humans. As we dare to read the Bible from cover to cover, we see so many situations and experiences which parallel what is taking place in our present world. This in itself is amazing! ARE YOU THE ONE?

Biblically speaking, there is a charge, a duty, a responsibility of every parent, child and human being that is given by God. If the charge is seriously accepted, it can reduce the hate and crimes which stare us in the face every day. All humans are 'created equal' by God when it comes to the love of which we are given and the faith to which each is given a measure. Parents are charged to train up their children in the way they should go (Proverbs 22:6 KJV). Children are charged to be obedient to their parents in the Lord (Ephesians 6:1 KJV), accepting their guidance, respecting them as disciplinarians who help them to develop and become responsible citizens. The commandment for children to obey their parents is actually the first commandment with promise (Exodus 20:12; Ephesians 6:2-3 KJV) Husbands are charged to love their wives as Christ loved the church and gave Himself up for the church (Ephesians 5:25, KJV). Wives are charged to submit and obey their own husbands, as unto the Lord (Ephesians 5:22 KJV). Don't toss this book into the fire after reading these passages. Instead think about them and ask yourself, where are the folk, where are the families who have accepted these charges? ARE YOU THE ONE?

Truth be told, we all have fallen short and missed the mark. Sin encamps at the door of our hearts. Delayed gratification, also known as discipline, has become a thing of the past in many lives. But I have hope that there is ONE who has chosen to live by the Bible and reap the harvest God planned. Don't forget that repentance and forgiveness are available for each of us, and we have opportunities to set our lives in order. We must contend, fight for our families, our spouses, and our children. When we fight, God will fight alongside us and help us to create an atmosphere of peace and unity in our homes. When families stay committed to each other and committed to God, there is nothing that can destroy the family. No weapon formed against us shall prosper (Isaiah 54:17). When we submit ourselves to God and resist the devil, the devil will flee (James 4:7 KJV). When the bad thoughts attack us and the memories of the wrongs done to us rise, we must resort to think on the things God has charged us to think about; those things which are true, honest, just, and pure, lovely and of good report (Philippians 4:8 KJV). These things are characteristic of God who never changes. We must not give up. There will be times when we fail. But we must fail forward, remembering that repetition is how we learn. Faith comes by hearing and hearing by the WORD OF GOD, not just once but over and over again. Trust develops along with greater insight and confidence. So, what if you fall? Proverbs

24:16, KJV says, "For a just man falleth seven times, and riseth up again: but the wicked shall fall into mischief". Don't go into something expecting to fail, but if by chance you don't succeed the first time and you know that you are in relationship with God, keep on pressing forward for you are not alone and there is purpose in your place! ARE YOU THE ONE who will make a habit of never giving up on yourself or your family? The change, the healing you want to see in this world begins in YOU and your family. ARE YOU THE ONE? Intercede!

Change Your Words, Change Your World

Proverbs 4: 23 in the KJV tells us that we are to keep our heart with all diligence; for out of it are the issues of life. This means that we don't let everything get inside of us. We have heard folk say, especially some pastors, that it's not the water surrounding the boat or ship that sinks it, but it is the water that is allowed to get into the boat or ship that causes it to sink! Likewise, we are surrounded by all sorts of things and especially words. We **are** words wrapped in flesh! How many times have you been told that you were just like 'so and so', and 'so and so' was a good for nothing tramp? How many times have you been told you were ugly? How many times have you been told that you were poor? How many times have you been told that you were not good enough for a certain job or title? How many times have you been told that you would never amount to anything? How many times have you been told that you were crazy? How many times have you been told that you were special? How many times have you been told that you were beautiful? How many times have you been told that you are loved and appreciated? Get the picture? People may say things about you. You may say many things about yourself! The question is, how much of what is said about you or to you do you allow to get inside you? The difference between us as human beings, is what we let inside of us. The successful businessman who made poor grades in college was always told by significant others that he was smart and had a great head on his shoulders. His grandmother told him that he was going to be somebody special and encouraged him to stay focused on learning and doing the best he could with what he had to work with. He let those positive words be his and became a multi-millionaire and well-known philanthropist in his community.

The scripture lets us know that we can prevent things from getting inside our hearts, our very core. It is at our core where we are most sensitive. Our heart controls our mind, will, and emotions – our very soul. What the heart embraces as truth, the mind will support! If you are letting negative things in your heart, you will live a negative life and never achieve the greatness that God has put inside you that must mature and be nourished day by day. Therefore, we must always be dressed in the full armor of God which totally protects us, and God is our REAR GUARD. Read the whole chapter of Ephesians 6 in whatever version of the Bible you can find and apply it to your life. Repent of any sin and negative acts and wear the armor of God consistently.

Sample Prayer:

Dear God, make me an instrument of blessing to those around me. Give me words to say to others and to myself that will cause others and me to be more like You and to make the world a better place in which to live. Help me to live a life of joy with a clean and pure heart that You are proud of. Your joy is my strength and I choose to be Your servant fully armored of You that I may resist all evil that comes against me today and all the days of my life. May my life always bring You glory. In Jesus' name. Amen

Now, begin to make a list of positive statements and say them out loud, speaking over your life each day, letting the words enter your heart. And when logismoi come, attack them instantly with the WORD OF GOD! Here are some examples:

- Things happen for me, not to me.
- I am the righteousness of God.
- No weapon formed against me shall prosper.
- I am the head and not the tail, above and not beneath.
- I am a lender, not a borrower.
- I can do all things through Jesus Christ who gives me strength.
- I am a habitual encourager to others and myself.
- I am fearfully and wondrously made.
- I am healed by the stripes of Jesus.
- The blood of Jesus cleanses me daily.
- I am pure and holy.
- I am God's greatest miracle.
- I am the apple of God's eye

- I am better today than I was on yesterday.
- Whatever I put my hands to prospers.
- I reap what I sow, and I sow love, kindness, mercy, and grace.
- I am a successful in all that I do for the glory of God.
- I am a kingdompreneur.
- God is my Main Customer.
- I seek opportunities, not mere security.
- I am a 'me only', not a 'me too'.
- I am a winner, not a whinner.
- I am loved and appreciated.
- I am patient and kind.
- I walk humbly before the Lord.
- I am worth fighting for.
- My life is worth living.
- I have something great to offer this world.
- I hunger and thirst for righteousness.
- I am made perfect in Christ Jesus.
- I am confident.
- I am courageous.
- I am creative.
- I am accepted of God.

- I am free to be me in Jesus.
- I will not trade freedom for beneficence.
- I am a giver.
- I am generous.
- I am made in God's image.
- I am who God says I am.
- I have a home in Heaven.
- I am faithful.
- I hope in God.
- I am resourceful.
- I acknowledge God in all of my ways, and He directs my steps.
- I am called according to God's purpose.
- I am disciplined and have control of my emotions.
- I choose to forgive others and myself.
- I declare and decree that the blood of Jesus covers me and removes all sin, hurt, and shame far from me.
- I choose to obey God's Word.
- I am wise.
- I am a good sibling.
- I am a good friend.
- I am a good spouse.

- I am a good citizen.
- I am a good parent.
- I am a peace maker.
- I am a child of God.
- I am a world changer.
- Great is the peace of my children for they are taught of the Lord.
- I am _____ (YOU fill in the blank)

ARE YOU THE ONE?

Rightly Dividing The Word of Truth

Jesus said in John 8:32 that "ye shall know the truth, and the truth shall make your free". To be free is a promise given to us by God when we come to know the truth. Unfortunately, the world's view of truth has become so tainted with lies and deception that if we don't diligently search the scriptures, we will never find the freedom that truth brings. Let's look at some basic proven truths which are derived from the Bible:

1. God is Light and in Him there is no darkness.
2. We are never alone, for God has promised never to leave us alone.
3. God's character is constant, He never changes.
4. God's grace is sufficient for us all.
5. God is love and we are made in His image.

6. We can love ourselves and our neighbors just as much.
7. God is God and besides Him there is no other God.
8. God is a Spirit, and we must worship Him in Spirit and in truth.

Everyone who is of the truth listens to the voice of Jesus who came into the world to bear witness unto the truth. Every one that is of the truth hears Jesus' voice (John 18:37, KJV). All scripture is inspired by God and is God breathed, meaning every word of God spoken in the scriptures whether directly, indirectly, through parables or straight-forward is the truth and undeniably GOD! God creates all things good and perfect, pure, and holy. It is the lust of man's heart that causes corruption and confusion which is all a part of the enemy's plan to steal, kill, and destroy (John 10:10 KJV).

Because we are born in the image of God, it is in our nature to want to know the truth; however, because of man's fallen nature, there is resistance to the truth.

Therefore, we must intentionally decide to follow God's way and be led by the Holy Spirit in order not to fulfill the lusts, gluttony, greed, laziness, wrath, envy, and pride which lie waiting at the doors of our hearts for the opportunity to take hold of our mind, will, and emotions. For this reason, Jesus tells us that we must be born again for it is then, and only then that we will be able to experience the Kingdom of God and live the eternal life we were created to live (John 3:3 KJV). If you never have done so, ask Jesus to come and live in your heart right now. If you have asked Him in the past but strayed away, return to God, and ask for forgiveness of your sins. Acknowledge that Jesus is still waiting for you to follow Him and He wants YOU to decide to get back on track. TRUST GOD!

The light which radiates from God who is Light, helps us to see the darkness in our lives that must be removed. The GLORY OF THE LORD SHINES BRIGHTLY! We become aware of what must be removed and then are compelled to seek God's guidance to change us and help us to live as we should. It is by grace that we are saved through faith in our Lord Jesus Christ. There is nothing in and of ourselves that we can actually DO to be saved, as in good deeds and treating others right, etc. but because we accept Jesus and activate our faith in Him, we find ourselves able to do justly, love mercy and walk humbly with God (Micah 6:8 KJV). Have you ever had an AH-HA moment where clarity hits you, the light bulb goes off/shines bright and you go eureka!!!!? Well, that is often what it's like when God reveals truth to you. And you may find yourself wanting more of the truth and nothing but the truth because with truth there is freedom! Don't spend time on the "coulda-, shoulda-, woulda-" rabbit hole. Just ask Jesus to help you with all the baggage, all the doubts, all the regrets, and let Him do the repairs as only He can!

In our broken world, truth requires great investigation, especially when related to business encounters and politics. Unfortunately, greed and the thirst for power can make some folks do ruthless things and behave as if they will never die.

They appear to live to suppress the free opportunities created for us all. It's just a doggone shame that so many people are blinded by lies and succumb to the character bashing and smear tactics of those who will do anything to make someone else look bad. Why? Because they are lazy, too lazy to search for the truth. The perfect truth can be found in the Life Manual called the Bible. Similar to the car manual, many folks do not open it until there is a problem and too often it may be too late. Of course, there are some who only look for something in the Bible to justify their behaviors and often take things out of context. The car manual MAY often get more attention but more likely than not, owners rely on the mechanics to solve the issues with the vehicles and still don't read their manuals. Likewise, some may tend to expect God's blessings without ever knowing the full richness of the promises they can find in His Word. These may be the church goers who just rely on the preacher to tell the truth but never use the Bible as the litmus test to see if what they are hearing is indeed truth! Hmmm... another ingredient for broken-ness. There is nothing new under the sun as has been said before so in the Bible you will find prophesy both spoken and fulfilled which reflects what is happening some-where in the world right now! We see the same games, same tactics, and even sometimes manipulation with lessons yet to be learned. Follow God's plan and you won't be deceived. Obey Him and as a child of God, you will never live in regret.

What a privilege it is to have God's presence and the sweet reassurance of knowing that God is always with us no matter what the situation. I remember my mother telling us whether we were about to go someplace with a friend or whether we were going to stay home alone, "God is with you, and He sees everything!" That would help us to be on our p's and q's, but only if we believed it. And of course, sometimes somebody would test the waters and consequences came swiftly! That is an issue in the world today. Too many people don't believe or have become calloused to the fact that no matter what we are doing or saying, God sees it all, knows our hearts and has the final say on the day of judgment. We arrogantly assume that God will give us another opportunity to right a wrong or do something that we were supposed to do anyway, at a later time, also known as procrastination. We are ALL guilty to some degree of abusing God's grace and mercy. This must cease if we are to have a better world. God deserves our extravagant respect and attention first, not as a side dish or second thought.

God is Love and His character never changes. We often disappoint Him and may be chastised by Him, but He is so patient, kind and loving and He gives us opportune time to come to Him and repent of our wrongs. One day, unexpectedly, that opportune time will be no longer, so it behooves us all to live each day in Christ as if it were our last, not in fear but in love. God is our CHIEF CUSTOMER, and we should do everything possible to please Him. My prayer on a daily basis is for God to have His way in me and change me so that I will please Him. When I lack wisdom about a thing, I must remember that He says I can ask Him, and He will freely give it to me and not take it back. Wisdom upon wisdom, precept upon precept, we **can** walk in a way that is pleasing to the Lord.

God's grace is sufficient for all of us and we must never forget that HE IS THE ALL SUFFICIENT ONE.   He has already provided everything we need and desire. What this means is that whatever God has for us, His impossible to be earned (by us) favor, His undying love, His provisions for our eternal life through Jesus Christ are more than enough to help us live our best lives and be the best "individually equipped to whip the devil" human beings, we can be! And we are stronger together!!! We are made in the image of God and the devil may not like it but there is NOTHING he can do about that fact. And the fact remains that the devil is already defeated! Because we can't always "see" God as we "see" the news on television or the headlines in the newspaper does not mean that He is not in control, and more than aware of the state of our world. Neither does it mean that He is not with us, for He has promised NEVER to leave or forsake us. He is waiting for us to acknowledge Him in all of our ways, in every situation so that He can do as He has promised, DIRECT OUR PATH! While it may sometimes seem that we are doomed and defeated, God wants us to assess ourselves, judge ourselves and determine what we have in our own hands to make the difference in this world and bring Him glory! When we change our words, we will change our world! Stop murmuring and complaining! When we learn to love, hate will disappear! When we realize who God really is, our perceptions about life will change for the better! When we worship God, giving Him extravagant praise and attention, the world will evolve into something beautiful, and His Kingdom will be in earth as it is in HEAVEN! The power of ONE is the strength of many. Know the truth and be free! The Word of God brings truth! God is TRUTH! TRUST GOD!

Are YOU THE ONE who will not only demand the truth but be truthful? ARE YOU

THE ONE who will reflect what we are told that this country was built on and is engraved in our currency, "In God We Trust"? Perhaps when the decision was made to engrave this statement on our currency, folk didn't understand that the inspirational power of God was in action, yet today although no one seems to pay attention to that statement as they barter and trade, trust in God has never been more necessary. ARE YOU THE ONE who will open your talents and treasures before Jesus and favorably impact this world? You don't even have to leave your city or state. The corridor effect, the ripple effect, empowered by God will be released right where you are for there is yet another ONE nearby whom you may never personally know. And if by chance God tells you to move, DO IT AND DO IT WITHOUT HESITATION! OBEY GOD! Trust in God and BE THE ONE!

Choose Your Relationships With Care

We are not in this world to live in seclusion though there are occasions when we need to spend some time in solitude so that we can meditate, reflect, pray, read, talk to our Creator God, and receive clarity on what God has planned for us. We need to take time to rest, to breathe, to organize and prepare but we also need some form of relationship with others. This does not mean that we have to be chummy-chummy with everyone we meet but we must respect and acknowledge one another as human beings, created in the image of God with a purpose! Think about the fact that around 400 million sperm cells raced to enter one egg and that one egg became you! Wow! You are one of God's greatest miracles and you are **not** a mistake. And if you a twin or a product of multiple births, just remember without a doubt that you are a God's miracle! You are privileged to enjoy the company of other miracles, but each miracle has choices to make.

Proverbs13:20 KJV tells us, "He that walketh with wise men shall be wise: but a companion of fools shall be destroyed." Not everyone will believe in God regardless of the fact that He created us all in His image. There are those who proclaim to be atheist, believing not in the God of our salvation. The fool hath said in his heart, there is no God (Psalm 14:1 KJV). Therefore, it is of utmost importance that we choose our friends wisely and teach our loved ones to do the same. Pray for God to open your eyes so that you can make the changes you need to make and ask Him to give you the courage to distance yourself from people who try to drag you down. John 10:10 KJV says, "the thief cometh not, but for to steal, and to kill, and to destroy I(Jesus) am come that they might have life, and that they might have it more abundantly". Jesus came to give us abundant life and we must not be entangled with those who do not believe in Him. Stop making soul ties with those who do not deserve to be a part of you. You are not your own. You belong to God and when you choose to go out of His will to bond with someone whom He has not approved for you, you will not like the consequences. This does not mean that we think of ourselves as better than anyone else and stick our noses up or look down on people. No, we don't do that, but we pray for one another. We are to be an example, a reflection of Jesus. We are still kind and compassionate, but we are not involved in a bond that is not in God's plan for us. Win a friend over to the way of Jesus by your example, lifting Jesus up daily through Your actions. Your actions speak loudly.

Thank God for blessing you with wonderful Christian friends and do your best to be a blessing to others every day. Show love and generosity as an example of a loving God. We need one another. We must help each other to be the best Christians possible, fighting for the greatest good of each other in every situation to the glory of God! Pray that God will make you an instrument of blessing to those around you and give you self-control to hold your tongue when you are tempted to speak negatively. Choose to have a positive life full of joy that is reflected in what you say and what you do. This should be evident in your home as well as place of employment and in the general community, for this affects our world. ARE YOU THE ONE?

Sometimes we get upset and may become offended by what another person does or does not do. Relationships are not always easy to maintain and grow. Relationships require work, effort! Selflessness, forgiveness, respect, and communication are among the requirements in a relationship that is to last and be in God's will. With God, it is possible to forgive and forget past hurts and release bitterness, and resentment. I am a witness to how difficult it can be to overcome heartbreak, especially when it hits home, and a family member hurts you to the point where you no longer want to be a part of the family. But if reconciliation is at all possible, one must put forth the effort because that is God's will. When we practice these types of behaviors in the family arena, it is easier to transfer these practices wherever we go. As someone pointed out to me on more than one occasion, family is not only those who share the same maternal or paternal blood; but in Christ, we share the saving blood and therefore are FAMILY!

One last thought in this book (which may become a series) is ask God to help you love. Do you measure up to the litmus test of love as found in 1 Corinthians 13 (NIV):

- Love (charity) is patient.
- Love is kind.
- Love does not envy.
- Love does not boast.
- Love is not proud.
- Love is not self-seeking.
- Love is not easily angered.
- Love keeps no record of wrongs.
- Love does not delight in evil.
- Love rejoices with the truth.
- Love always protects.
- Love always trusts.
- Love always hopes.
- Love always perseveres.
- Love never fails.

It's safe to say that we all have work to do and if we focus on improving our personal love walk every day, we can affirmatively say:

- Our home life will be better today.
- Our work life will be better today.
- Our community will be better today.
- Our world will be better today.
- I AM BETTER TODAY!

Sample Prayer

Lord, it's hurtful and I know it. The words I have spoken to others don't always come out right and it's hurtful to them and to me. It's not pleasing to you either Lord. Forgive me and please give me the strength of character to show mercy to others by not spreading or delighting in their bad news or faults. Help me to always be loving and kind. Remove iniquity far from me and grant peace to me, my home and every area of my life and make me an instrument of YOUR peace wherever I go. Thank You Father

God. Help me to be the ONE who makes You smile each day of my life. In Jesus' name. AMEN

ARE YOU THE ONE?

Be the change you want to see,
In this broken world
Let healing be-
In Your hand as boldly, your movements make-
Transforming lives, destroying hate.
Will you, a 'me only' and not a 'me too'
Make the world a better place
For me and you?
ARE YOU THE ONE?

Reflections/Visions

Reflections/Visions

Reflections/Visions

_____

_____

_____

_____

_____

_____

_____

_____

_____

_____

_____

_____

_____

_____

Reflections/Visions

_____

_____

_____

_____

_____

_____

_____

_____

_____

_____

_____

_____

_____

Reflections/Visions

_____

_____

_____

_____

_____

_____

_____

_____

_____

_____

_____

_____

_____

Lydia F. Best

Reflections/Visions

_____

_____

_____

_____

_____

_____

_____

_____

_____

_____

_____

_____

_____

47

Reflections/Visions

_____

_____

_____

_____

_____

_____

_____

_____

_____

_____

_____

_____

_____

_____

Reflections/Visions

_____

_____

_____

_____

_____

_____

_____

_____

_____

_____

_____

_____

_____

Reflections/Visions

About the Author

Rev. Dr. Lydia Best is a health care professional with myriad experiences obtained through her formal training as a Registered Nurse, Family Nurse Practitioner, Certified Lifestyle Coach, Diabetes Care Specialist as well as her experiences as an Associate Professor of Nursing, and Commander in the United States Navy Nurse Corps. She is a graduate of the Hollingsworth's B.O.S.S. Master's Program where she is now a coach to youth ages 6-1/2 to 11-1/2 who are becoming successful leaders, actualizing their birthrights, achieving their dreams, and learning what it means to have God-confidence. As an Ordained Minister, Entrepreneur and CEO of Inspired To Be Ministries, Dr. Best is committed to service in her church and community and various forms of outreach. Impactful and inspiring, Dr. Best challenges others to learn who they are, whose they are and identify their role(s) in making purposeful actions toward experiencing and living in the best possible world. Married to

her high school sweetheart, Dennis for 45
years, they are proud parents of Malcolm Sr.
and Marcus Sr. and blessed grandparents of
8 wonderful grandchildren.

Made in the USA
Columbia, SC
20 June 2023

18015168R00037